Children and Holy Communion

A creative preparation programme

Diana Murrie and Steve Pearce

kevin
mayhew

First published in Great Britain in 2003 by Kevin Mayhew Ltd
Buxhall, Stowmarket, Suffolk IP14 3BW

Tel: +44 (0) 1449 737978 Fax: +44 (0) 1449 737834

E-mail: info@kevinmayhewltd.com

www.kevinmayhew.com

9 8 7 6 5 4 3 2 1 0

ISBN 978 1 84417 151 4
Catalogue No 1500639

Cover design by Rob Mortonson
Layout and illustrations by Chris Coe

Printed and bound in Great Britain

Contents

For Isabella

A Message from the Archbishop of Canterbury

Baptised children no less than adults have their spiritual lives fortified and enriched by sharing in Holy Communion; and the experience of many parishes in recent decades has underlined the great gifts that can be brought into the common life of the Christian community by encouraging baptised children to take a full part in the assembly that celebrates the Lord's Supper.

Happily, the Church of England now recognises the importance of this in the structures of its Canon Law. Those who have taken advantage of the provisions thus made available have been able to explore their understanding of the Sacrament in fresh ways, and in many cases to discover a renewed commitment to the mystery of Holy Communion on the part of adult and younger believers alike.

But to help children to know more about Holy Communion and to prepare them to receive it prayerfully requires a creative approach to nurture and resources. I am delighted that this book is appearing in a fresh edition, once more revised and updated, to give churches tested and valuable material to use with their younger members as they prepare for and share in Communion and look forward also to Confirmation. I am very happy to commend it warmly, in the hope that it will be widely and creatively used.

† ROWAN WILLIAMS

About the Authors

Diana Murrie was the Church of England's National Children's Officer for over ten years. Previously she was Head of Prayer and Spirituality at the Mothers' Union, after having served as Children's Adviser in the Diocese of Bristol. She retired in 2006 and now lives in Somerset.

Steve Pearce now works in the World Church Relationships Office of the British Methodist Church, looking after Asia and the Pacific. He was formerly their Secretary for Children's Work, after many years as Children's Work Adviser in the Anglican Dioceses of Derby, Lincoln and Southwell.

Acknowledgements

Many of the ideas in this book, especially in the preparation sessions, come from the children, preparation group leaders and clergy of parishes in the Southwell Diocese and from their representatives meeting as the Children And Communion Monitoring Group.

We extend our thanks for the pioneering work and dedication of the following parishes:

All Saints, Huthwaite

St Peter and St Paul, Hucknall

All Hallows, Ordsall, Retford

Bestwood Park and Rise Park,
 Anglican Methodist LEP, Bestwood

St James, Porchester, Nottingham

St Martin, Sherwood, Nottingham

St John the Divine, Bulwell, Nottingham

Thanks also to the children who tried out the Talkabout sheets for us at

St Michael the Archangel, Sittingbourne

PART ONE

History and Background

The History and the Reports

It seems clear that children were present in the earliest Christian communities and were initiated into the faith along with adults. There is, of course, no explicit mention of any special approach to the baptism of children in the New Testament. They were included with the family or household, and there is certainly no mention of any baptised members being excluded from the celebration of the Eucharist. So for children, as for anyone else, membership of the Church is obtained by baptism and thereafter depends on continuing participation in the Eucharist.

> The completing of John 3:5 '. . . unless one is born of water and the Spirit, he cannot enter the kingdom of God . . .' with John 6:53 '. . . unless you eat the flesh of the Son of Man and drink his blood, you have no life in you' establishes what is necessary for participation in the Christian community.
> *Communion before Confirmation, page 8*

From a certain perspective, the history of children and Communion in the West in later centuries can be described as a story of children losing their place at the central table of the community, having to wait many years for a reasoned explanation of why this should have been done to them, and then being made to wait as long again for their counter-arguments in favour of reinstatement to be heard and accepted. In the East the right and need of children to receive Communion is unquestioned.

In detail, the historical exploration discovers a variety of practices and a variety of justifications follow changes in the practice. In broad terms, though, the changes in our tradition came about in this way.

During the medieval period, for a variety of reasons, baptism, Confirmation and admission to Communion came to be seen as separate events. Three of the reasons are briefly outlined below. They were largely pragmatic and a theological justification, for the newer pattern was only developed later, after changes had taken place.

First, while Augustine was clear that children needed to receive Communion as much as adults did, his doctrine of 'original sin' encouraged the notion that infants should be baptised as early as possible, to secure their future in heaven. The growing size of dioceses meant that the bishop only visited every few years and it became impossible for him as the minister of baptism and laying on of hands/anointing to meet the needs of the population. The problem was solved by allowing a local minister to perform the water and signing of the cross part of the baptism, and waiting for the visit of the bishop for the laying on of hands. Admission to Communion, though, was still associated with the priest's performance of the baptism, not with the bishop's laying on of hands.

Second, there was a growing tradition of the 'real' nature of the consecrated elements in the Eucharist, which demanded such 'care' that the laity were denied the wine and given only bread and children sometimes denied altogether.

Third, a regulation issued by Archbishop Peckham at the Council of Lambeth in 1281, that those not confirmed (without good reason) should be barred from Communion was an attempt to counter the 'damnable negligence' of parents who failed to present their children to the bishop for laying on of hands/anointing, rather than the expression of any theological or spiritual insight. The practice of communicating unconfirmed adults and children was finally abolished at the Council of Trent in the sixteenth century.

During the Reformation instruction and understanding became significant concepts in deciding who should receive Communion. Cranmer's Prayer Book of 1549 stated: 'There shall none be admitted to the Holy Communion, until such time as he can say the Catechism, and be confirmed.' This emphasised the understanding, which should presumably follow from learning the Catechism, rather than the formal rite of Confirmation.

> It seems that from the sixteenth century to the nineteenth the great preponderance of Anglican communicants were admitted to Communion not on the basis of being confirmed, but of having been baptised and having received some minimal instruction from the parochial incumbent.
>
> *Communion before Confirmation*

In the nineteenth century Confirmation developed into the familiar 'gateway to Communion' and twentieth-century Anglicans came to believe that it had always been the precondition for receiving the sacrament.

In 1969 the Ely Commission was asked to reconsider questions of initiation and reported in *Christian Initiation: Birth and Growth in the Christian Society* (CIO, 1971), concluding that baptism is complete sacramental initiation and that adults and children should be admitted to Holy Communion on that basis. After reporting on the report and referring the matter to dioceses, in 1976 the General Synod decided with a 60/40 majority not to proceed to a change in the admission of children to Communion.

The minority was nevertheless large and various semi-official 'experiments' were underway. Synod returned to the issue in the early 1980s and the Knaresborough Report was published as *Children and Communion*. It recommended that regulations for the admission of baptised people to Holy Communion should be drawn up and approved. Synod 'took note' in November 1985 but did nothing further. In 1991, however, a report from the House of Bishops on initiation was discussed and Synod accepted the bishops' motion to permit early Confirmation, but rejected one asking to discontinue 'experiments of admission to Communion before Confirmation'. A 1993 report on three 'experimental' dioceses (Manchester, Peterborough and Southwark) found a substantial majority of the parishes concerned were 'convinced of the positive value of admitting children before Confirmation'.

In 1995, the report *On the Way* was published with encouragement to parishes to review their patterns of initiation and consider various options, including the admission of children to Communion at an earlier age, reserving Confirmation as a rite of adult commitment and beginning of adult ministry around the age of 18. The guidelines from the House of Bishops on the admission of children to Communion were published in 1996 and welcomed by Synod in November of that year. The guidelines were slightly modified in January 1997, following the debate in Synod, and implemented. Finally, in 2005, the House of Bishops recommended that the issue was too important to be governed merely by Guidelines and therefore needed firmer legislation. In 2006, General Synod agreed to bring the Guidelines into Canon Law by making them Regulations, cited as the Admission of Baptised Children to Holy Communion Regulations 2006, under paragraph 1(c) of Canon B15A. They are reprinted here on pages 12 and 13.

This process in the Church of England is mirrored in many other denominations and in other parts of the Anglican Communion. Methodist and United Reformed Church congregations, for instance, have been encouraged for some years now to welcome children to the Lord's Table; the Methodist Church in Britain now describes it as 'normative' that baptised children should receive Communion. The Anglican churches in Australia, Canada, New Zealand, South Africa and the United States have already made it possible for Communion to follow baptism before Confirmation. Meanwhile Roman Catholic practice in most places is for children to have their first Communion around the age of 7, and the Eastern Orthodox churches have always acknowledged the need of children to receive Holy Communion from baptism onwards.

The convincing arguments in favour of a change in practice seem to have been:

- the nature of baptism.
- the acceptance of children in the Church.
- children's need for spiritual nourishment.
- children's need to belong.
- the need of adults to become 'as a child'.

The bishops address the nature of baptism in these terms: 'The entire profession of the

Christian life . . . is represented in the action of baptism.' (House of Bishops GS 1212). In other words, baptism makes us full members of the Body of Christ.

It is on the basis of that baptism that we are therefore bidden to express our membership in the receiving of the bread and the wine at Holy Communion. To exclude the children is to deny their baptism.

Jesus' acceptance of children was explicit and particular:

> They brought children for him to touch. The disciples rebuked them, but when Jesus saw this he was indignant, and said to them, 'Let the children come to me, do not try to stop them; for the kingdom of God belongs to such as these. And he put his arms round them, laid his hands upon them, and blessed them.
>
> *Mark 10:13, 14, 16*

The Church is being challenged to be as welcoming and accepting of children as Jesus was.

Children's need for spiritual nurture is often interpreted as a requirement to teach a body of knowledge or an explicit moral code; far more is required, however. Children grow up as members of communities, assimilating the values and habits of the adults around them as well as of their peer group. We can teach them whatever we like about being a Christian, but their experience of the Christian people around them will far outweigh what they have been told. Similarly their experience of the Christian life, the joy of fellowship with other Christians, the excitement of the great festivals, the support in time of need and the regular pattern of encounter with God in prayer and sacrament will all become part of the fabric of their lives in a way that what they are just told about will not.

We all need to belong, and seldom stay in a place or group if we feel we don't belong there. This is especially true for children, who increasingly have the experience of leaving groups that don't meet their needs. Children in the 7 – 11 age group have a great enjoyment of being part of a group, in particular one which contains adults too. It is an age when they will feel keenly any action which denies their membership or fails to include them. At this time they need to be active participants in those activities which define the group so that any exclusion must be very clearly thought out and well understood if the church community is not to reap in teenage years the lack of involvement and poor quality of relationship sown in these crucial earlier years.

> 'I tell you, whoever does not accept the kingdom of God like a child will never enter it.'
>
> *Mark 10:15*

Jesus challenges us not only to welcome children wholeheartedly into the Church, but also to cherish the way they belong to the Kingdom and to be like them. It is the experience of many who have knelt at the altar in the presence of children, that these words strike home keenly and take on a powerful resonance.

Admission of Baptised Children to Holy Communion Regulations 2006

The General Synod hereby makes the following Regulations under paragraph 1(c) of Canon B15A:

1. These Regulations may be cited as the Admission of Baptised Children to Holy Communion Regulations 2006 and shall come into force on the fifteenth day of June 2006 as appointed by the Archbishops of Canterbury and York.

2. Children who have been baptised but who have not yet been confirmed and who are not yet ready and desirous to be confirmed as required by paragraph 1(a) of Canon B15A may be admitted to Holy Communion provided that the conditions set out in these Regulations are satisfied.

3. Every diocesan bishop may at any time make a direction to the effect that applications from parishes under these Regulations may be made in his diocese. The bishop's discretion in this respect shall be absolute, and he may at any time revoke such a direction (without prejudice to the validity of any permissions already granted thereunder).

4. Where a direction under paragraph 3 is in force in a diocese, an incumbent may apply to the bishop for permission that children falling within the definition of paragraph 2 may be admitted to Holy Communion in one or more of the parishes in the incumbent's charge. Such application must be made in writing and must be accompanied by a copy of a resolution in support of the application passed by the parochial church council of each parish in respect of which the application is made.

5. Before granting any permission under paragraph 4, the bishop must first satisfy himself (a) that the parish concerned has made adequate provision for preparation and continuing nurture in the Christian life and will encourage any child admitted to Holy Communion under these Regulations to be confirmed at the appropriate time and (b) where the parish concerned is within the area of a local ecumenical project established under Canon B44, that the other participating Churches have been consulted.

6. The bishop's decision in relation to any application under paragraph 4 shall be final, but a refusal shall not prevent a further application being made on behalf of the parish concerned, provided that at least one year has elapsed since the most recent previous application was refused.

7. Any permission granted under paragraph 4 shall remain in force unless and until revoked by the bishop. The bishop must revoke such permission upon receipt of an application for the purpose made by the incumbent. Such application must be made in writing and accompanied by a copy of a resolution in support of the application passed by the parochial church council of each parish in respect of which the application is made. Otherwise, the bishop may only revoke a permission granted under paragraph 4 if he considers that the conditions specified in paragraph 5 are no longer being satisfactorily discharged. Before revoking any permission on these grounds, the bishop shall first notify the incumbent of his concerns in writing and shall afford the incumbent a reasonable time to respond and, where appropriate, to take remedial action.

8. Where a permission granted under paragraph 4 is in force, the incumbent shall not admit any child to Holy Communion unless he or she is satisfied that (a) the child has been baptised and (b) a person having parental responsibility for the child is content that the child should be so admitted. Otherwise, subject to any direction of the bishop, it is within the incumbent's absolute discretion to

decide whether, and if so when, any child should first be admitted to Holy Communion.

9. The incumbent shall maintain a register of all children admitted to Holy Communion under these Regulations, and where practicable will record on the child's baptismal certificate the date and place of the child's first admission. If the baptismal certificate is not available, the incumbent shall present the child with a separate certificate recording the same details.

10. A child who presents evidence in the form stipulated in paragraph 9 that he or she has been admitted to Holy Communion under these Regulations shall be so admitted at any service of Holy Communion conducted according to the rites of the Church of England in any place, regardless of whether or not any permission under paragraph 4 is in force in that place or was in force in that place until revoked.

11. These Regulations shall apply to a cathedral as if it were a parish, with the modifications that:

    (a) any application under paragraphs 3 or 7 must be made by the dean of the cathedral concerned, accompanied by a copy of the resolution in support of the application passed by the chapter of the cathedral concerned;

    (b) the obligations imposed on the incumbent under paragraphs 8 and 9 shall be imposed on the dean of the cathedral concerned.

12. A diocesan bishop may delegate any of his functions under these Regulations (except his functions under paragraph 3) to a person appointed by him for the purpose, being a suffragan or assistant bishop or archdeacon of the diocese.

13. In these Regulations:

    (a) 'incumbent', in relation to a parish, includes:

    (i) in a case where the benefice concerned is vacant (and paragraph (ii) below does not apply), the rural dean;

    (ii) in a case where a suspension period (within the meaning of the Pastoral Measure 1983) applies to the benefice concerned, the priest-in-charge; and

    (iii) in a case where a special cure of souls in respect of the parish has been assigned to a vicar in a team ministry by a Scheme under the Pastoral Measure 1983 or by licence from the bishop, that vicar; and

    (b) references to paragraph numbers are to the relevant paragraph or paragraphs in these Regulations.

Planning for Change in a Parish

On the Way, the report to the House of Bishops, outlined three patterns of initiation:

> Baptism; Confirmation as at present around the age of 12 to 14 years; Holy Communion.
>
> Baptism; Confirmation at an earlier age; Holy Communion.
>
> Baptism; Holy Communion; Confirmation in late teens.

Following the institution of the Regulations in June 2006, it is now open to each diocesan bishop to implement any or all of these patterns, as they see fit. Not all are doing it in the same way and it is important, in the first instance, to ascertain what the diocese expects and requires. Most information can be found on diocesan websites, or via the diocesan children's adviser. Many have produced information packs for parishes wishing to explore these issues.

Each pattern has different implications for the pattern of initiation, education and nurture of people of all ages. Many parishes will have taken their pattern of initiation for granted and may now wish to think through a coherent policy, which encompasses baptism, the welcome of young families, children's work, admission to Holy Communion, the style of youth work, Confirmation preparation, encouraging new adult members and supporting adult discipleship.

Because change has now taken place in the wider church, each local church will be affected in some way. Church members may be aware of the developments in the other denominations. New members of the congregation may bring experience of changed patterns of children's discipleship. If those new members include children, they may well be used to full participation in the Eucharistic life of the Church and rightly expect to be welcomed as communicant members. Every church therefore needs to reassess its practice in the light of these changes and new possibilities. Moving towards an informed decision, rather than relying on traditional understandings, may have its difficulties and diocesan advisers will be pleased to help parishes consider and evaluate the possible patterns.

Where there is some interest in considering a change in the pattern which is traditional in the parish, most of the following steps will need to be taken:

- Hold a discussion in the standing committee, leading to, if there is sufficient interest:
  - Some initial research referring to recent reports and diocesan policy and consultation with other parishes and advisers.
  - Conversations with local churches of other denominations about their policy and practice.
  - A substantial consideration at a PCC meeting, using a member or visiting adviser to take the lead on the item.
  - Time for members to pray, reflect and discuss with others.
- Further discussion and decision at a subsequent PCC meeting.
- In the event of a decision not to proceed, plan feedback to the congregation, pastoral strategy for those most affected and a review in due course.
- In the event of a decision to proceed, plan involvement of the whole congregation (see ideas in *Congregational Preparation and Learning,* pages 16 and 17).
- Consult with children's workers about a children's preparation programme.
- Select and train leaders for the preparation course.
- Consider the implications for the pattern of services, the liturgy and the participation of all ages.
- Communicate the planned arrangements to the bishop and to the whole congregation.

- Invite parents and children to declare an interest in receiving Communion.
- Give parents details of the new arrangements, the preparation course, ways they can help or be involved and maybe an invitation to a sociable learning or information occasion.
- Receive consent forms from parents.
- Plan and deliver the children's preparation course.
- Arrange the (annual) service at which children will receive Holy Communion for the first time.
- Record the names of all children admitted to Communion.
- Write letters of commendation to their new parish for any children who move.
- Ensure that Communion services meet the needs of all communicant and non-communicant participants.
- Arrange to review these procedures and their contribution to the life of the church.
- Join with other parishes in diocesan monitoring and evaluation process.

Congregational Preparation and Learning

If the children follow an exploration of the story and symbolism of the Holy Communion, it gives the whole congregation the opportunity to discover more too. It also highlights the responsibility of the adult members to help the younger ones by welcoming and talking to them, and so sharing their faith with them.

This learning project, *Children and Holy Communion,* provides a chance for the adult and children's learning groups to take the same topic and benefit from seeing and talking about each other's work. If the house group, the preachers, the youth group, the children's groups and the new communicants' group are all in some way taking Communion as their theme, the opportunities for the exchange of news and ideas in conversations, drama, display, etc. within the church, are enormous. An exchange of views in this area with Christians of other denominations may be a fruitful way of learning and taking ecumenical relations forward.

Ideas already tried include the following:

A service commentary

A commentary is prepared and delivered alongside the Sunday morning Eucharist. This takes the form of information about the function, history and theology of certain parts of the service and also pauses for meditation or personal reflection at one or two key points. It is best spoken by someone other than the celebrant positioned away from the action of the service. While the commentary will depend on one or two people with some theological information, it can also include questions and observations contributed by members of all ages.

Photo board: members of the Body

The children's study material suggests making a display which includes their names and photographs, this can be used by the rest of the congregation – especially the adults, to make a conscious effort to get to know them. It is often the case that the members of the Body of Christ in any one place don't know each other as well as they imagine, and could usefully join in such a display. Everyone could be asked to provide a photo (it might be just as easy to photograph people in small groups as they arrive or leave on Sunday) and add their name and two or three pieces of information about themselves. Then add group photos of the PCC, choir, local clergy, flower arrangers, etc. It is important that the board is noticed, and since people will always look at any photos on them, the more faces that are included, the better.

Prayer

If the children are learning about Communion, pray for them by name during the Communion service and give adults a list of their names to use in their daily prayer. Ask the children in their session to remember in prayer those adults to be mentioned by name in church that day.

Wonder with the children

One church used the occasion of the children's first Communion to ask them questions such as: 'What do you think about when you are going to the altar to receive Holy Communion, and when you go back to your seat?' and: 'What do you like about Communion?' The answers included comments such as: 'Going up to the altar is like going with Jesus as he carried his cross,' and: 'Afterwards it is like coming back from the empty tomb!' In the children's group or at home use open, wondering questions with the children such as: 'I wonder what you think about/like/feel when . . .' Then give the children opportunity to express that wondering in paint, clay, poetry or prose.

The Christian understanding of Communion has always had something to say to local and wider communities about the way we 'live his risen life' both individually and in community, and it may be appropriate to learn and reflect about Communion with one eye open to the opportunities in your locality to share the learning outside the church as well as inside. The local school may be able to use a contribution from you in an assembly or within the work of the RE department. You may be moved to 'bring life to others' by taking up a campaigning issue on behalf of people who are at the disadvantaged end of our unequal society either in Britain or internationally. A community need might be met or a project nourished towards success by an input of church people, time, talents, money or buildings.

> . . . May we who share Christ's body live his risen life;
> we who drink this cup bring life to others;
> we whom the Spirit lights give light to the world.
> Keep us firm in the hope you have set before us,
> so we and all your children shall be free . . .
>
> *Common Worship: Services and Prayers for the Church of England, page 265*

Preparing Children for Communion

The essential requirements for the admission of a child to Holy Communion might be summarised like this:

- The child must be baptised and regularly attend church.
- The child should themselves wish to receive Communion.
- There must be some parental or adult support.
- There must be some preparation before admission to Communion.

The local church in welcoming children into the fellowship of the eucharistic meal also takes on responsibilities:

- To provide a warm and continuing welcome to children at services of Holy Communion.
- To ensure the liturgy of the main celebration of Holy Communion is appropriate for all ages.
- To provide financial and human resources for the preparation of children.
- To allow opportunity for children to use their gifts and develop their ministry, encouraging them in due course to come to Confirmation and a commitment to adult discipleship.

The parents of each child should have the opportunity to be involved in some way, both at the beginning of the preparation process and in the service when the child is to receive Communion for the first time. Some preparation groups have invited parents to join in the sessions and this has sometimes worked well. Other groups have found the children's conversation to be inhibited by the presence of parents and invited them to join the group for only one special meeting. Leaders will have to make their own judgement on this, and perhaps try different patterns before finally deciding on the best way to do it.

In the main, parishes have set up a special group for the preparation course, meeting away from Sunday groups, usually mid-week after school or in the early evening. This helps the group to form and see itself as doing something special. It also makes it easier to identify the commitment (from children and parents) of attending all the meetings.

A visit or letter to the parents/carers will be necessary initially, for the purpose of:

- Checking that they are happy with their child's decision to receive Holy Communion.
- Explaining, if necessary, the change in practice that has occurred in the pattern of Baptism, Holy Communion and Confirmation.
- Checking that the child is baptised, and if necessary, explaining that those who aren't baptised already, will be baptised before receiving Communion.
- Giving details of the preparation course, dates, times, leaders, materials required etc., and the expectation of attendance at all the sessions. These are best in written form with a tear-off consent form.
- Clarifying the implications for parents of the commitment to regular attendance on Sundays that their child is making.
- Inviting them to the service when the children will receive Communion for the first time.

A get-together for children and parents who are considering joining the preparation arrangements could usefully be held some weeks before it begins. It could then include much of the agenda above and one or two of the learning activities from the course itself, giving people a flavour of the course and allowing them time to become familiar with the pattern and details – such as co-operating over delivery and collection of the children. Session 1, *Belonging to God*, contains sufficient choice of learning activities for you to plan an introductory session (a Saturday morning or a Sunday afternoon perhaps) for the children, with their parents, sponsors, clergy and interested members of the congregation either instead of, or as well as a session with the children on their own.

Experience shows that while the children are thinking and learning about Holy Communion, their parents will also be doing some re-thinking and may well enjoy opportunities to discuss what the children are doing and what they think about it all.

The Talkabout take-home sheets will give children and parents a chance to talk at home about some of the issues raised.

As children begin to receive Holy Communion on a Sunday this will change their relationship with the rest of the congregation. Children and young people depend on their relationship with the adults in their church for their continuing involvement in its life and it is worth encouraging these relationships to grow at this opportune moment. Session 1 suggests a display in church of photographs, names and interests. This idea could be developed to include others. Some parishes have developed the idea of 'sponsors'. An adult is chosen for each child, and their responsibility is to pray for them, take an interest in them as they work through the preparation course, perhaps take a role when they first receive Communion – and after that the relationship will probably develop on its own.

The service at which children receive Holy Communion for the first time will be a very special occasion for them. They may well remember it for a long time to come, so it is worth giving it some serious thought and careful planning. In the main, parishes find it best to decide on an appropriate time of year for this event and then keep to that date on an annual basis. Common dates to choose are Easter, All Saints, Advent Sunday or the patronal festival. The liturgy should be that normally used for a celebration of Holy Communion, but with contributions from the children themselves and from their preparation sessions. It can be a day for children and young people to take responsibility for as many of the tasks of the day as possible, doing the readings, leading the prayers, giving out books, taking the offertory, making and serving refreshments, arranging flowers, contributing drama, music, story etc. Children can be encouraged to invite godparents, grandparents, friends and their wider family. It is a good idea for the church to present each child with a card or a gift to mark the occasion. When it comes to the Communion itself the children might gather round the altar for the Eucharistic prayer, or come up at the invitation and be the first to receive.

Anxieties Addressed

There are many convincing reasons for the admission of children to Holy Communion and plentiful stories of benefits to children and congregations but most parishes, or at least some of their members, foresee at least one or two problems arising when the pattern changes. These anxieties often highlight issues of real concern and must be addressed if the church is to cope creatively with the change. The most commonly expressed worries are detailed below.

The children don't really understand

It is not easy to shake off the notion that the point at which people should begin to receive Holy Communion is the point at which they 'understand'. A variety of insights give pause for thought here. Adults don't understand either. Receiving Communion contributes to our lives, to our bodies, minds and spirits in some ways that we understand and in others that we don't come to understand for many years, if at all. We don't apply this requirement of 'understanding' to adults with learning difficulties. Children don't need to understand; they need to belong and receive God's grace. We come to Holy Communion not because of what we know but because we are invited. Any one of these thoughts may help individuals to reflect further on their own understanding of what Holy Communion is and does for them and what it could be and do for children.

The children won't be serious or reverent enough

This fear is voiced or lurks silently in most parishes contemplating the admission of children to Communion. In practice the children identify with the intrinsic importance of the occasion and behave appropriately. They also identify with the mood of the rest of the congregation and conform to the behaviour of the adults around them. In short, it does not turn out to be a problem. Things to avoid, however, are children sitting in bunches on their own (split them up into family size groups with adult members of the congregation); and children at the back of the church or in places where they can't see or hear (draw them into the midst).

Confirmation will disappear

Many of us have for some time felt that Confirmation of the 10 – 13 age group has been largely serving as a 'passing out parade' rather than as personal commitment and a gateway to Christian ministry. While Church statistics show the proportion of adult Confirmations has increased, as those of children and young people have declined, its power and potential have become clearer. In 1976 the 12 – 15 age range held nearly 60 per cent of all candidates, while the 20-and-over age group was less than 20 per cent. By 1996 this had changed. Adult confirmations had risen to just over 50 per cent while numbers in the 12 – 15 age group had dropped to just over 30 per cent.

Rather than Confirmation diminishing if children are admitted to Communion on the basis of their baptism, it is to be hoped and expected that we will, as a church, make more of it as an occasion of transition to adulthood at 16 or 17, when it can mark the beginning of adult discipleship and affirm the signs of the individual's Christian ministry.

What about children who aren't baptised?

Baptism always precedes admission to Holy Communion and this is reaffirmed in the Regulations. Unbaptised children usually come from one of two categories – those whose parent/carers did not see baptism as a priority, and those who decided to wait until their baby was older.

It is important when children from the first category decide they wish to join a group to prepare to receive Holy Communion that effective consultation takes place with the family and that full understanding and agreement is reached about the baptism, particularly if the family are not church attenders.

Where the family are church attenders and therefore more likely to fall into the second category, it is even more important that the child takes part in the consultation. Recognition of a discernment of the significance of Holy Communion, however inadequately expressed, is the beginning of a personal journey of faith and commitment.

It is our understanding of baptism that is leading the Church of England to accept the diversity of practice, which now includes Communion before Confirmation. The baptism of a child marks their entry into membership of the Body of Christ and s/he is sustained in that membership by participation in Holy Communion.

The baptism of an unbaptised child should become part of the preparation to receive Holy Communion. It can be referred to in Session 2 of the course and can form a creative part of the service in which the child's first reception of Communion is marked in a suitable way before the whole congregation.

We won't know who has been prepared and admitted and who hasn't

The admission to Communion remains a formal process and the Regulations point out that a record should be kept of the names of children who are prepared and admitted. The importance of getting to know the children is highlighted here, especially for those who assist with the administration of Communion.

Is everyone happy with the change?

As with any change, particularly in the church where we are dealing with things dear to our hearts, it is important to share information and opinions. The change has been most successfully managed in parishes which have been careful to learn about the relevant issues, listen in an open way to each other's responses and express their own views clearly. Listening to a visitor from a parish that has already changed is a common and successful approach. It means that people hear for themselves that things can be different and still as good – a reassuring experience.

It is divisive, some receive and some don't

Seeing that some of your friends go to the altar to receive Communion, does emphasise the fact that you don't, but more importantly it raises the 'why' and 'how' questions. Those children who now receive Communion are often given confidence by this clear sign of their belonging, and some individuals clearly see their church going in a more positive light now that they are communicant members. It is in fact an evangelistic opportunity, a demonstration of the possibilities and the demands of commitment and belonging, not a worry.

This is yet another erosion of childhood

There is no loss of childhood here. Communion is not essentially an adult activity, rather an open-handed, trusting acceptance of grace. No child is free from the stresses of living in this world, and participation in Holy Communion can help them cope too.

Some Stories from Pioneer Parishes

The parishes from which these stories come have between four and twenty years' experience of admitting children to Communion before Confirmation.

You've forgotten me

'You've forgotten me,' was the loud whisper of the shy young girl, who seldom offered more than two words to anyone at church, but being missed out at the Communion rail was more important by far than her usual shyness. 'You've forgotten me, Beverley, I take Communion now.' A repentant curate returned to give the bread, which was of an importance she could only guess at.

Taking prayers to school

Taking a full part in the central action of your church gives some children a natural confidence in their faith and an unassuming desire to share its excitement with their friends. One example of this occurred when Ruth wrote a prayer in one of the preparation sessions. She was rightly pleased with what she had produced and took it to school with her and asked if it could be used in assembly one day. A small event in itself, but a pointer to the way membership of and support from the faith community can help children be confident in themselves as Christians, not just as children who are tolerated in a church on Sundays.

Introducing . . . our children

I was present one Advent Sunday at a thriving inner-city church, when the first group of children was to begin receiving Holy Communion. Before the Peace, the clergywoman who had led the preparation group called the children to the chancel step and began to introduce each child to the congregation. I momentarily froze at the patronising process which might follow, but, like the rest of the congregation and the children themselves, swiftly warmed and smiled at the obviously caring and perceptive comments that were made. The rock, the joker and the treasure chest each recognised the thumb-nail sketch of the person they were, felt loved and, as they took the Peace to the other members of the Body of Christ in that place, they knew themselves to be valuable to God.

I went home thinking what a good, but what a difficult thing to do, and fell to wondering how I would like to be introduced to my congregation.

When you introduce children, it is helpful to:

- Check with them what you will say.
- Not lumber them with a nickname or symbol they will hate.
- Value each child equally.
- Present your glimpse of their gifts (not the ultimate truth about them).
- Do it lightly and lovingly.

Is it time yet?

Parish initiation schemes have, so far, included preparation for Holy Communion around the age of 7. There is some debate about the age, which many feel reflects a residual need to include cognitive understanding in the equation somewhere as well as more practical issues. Individual children occasionally make a nonsense of specific age limits, as in the case which follows. Such stories challenge adult expectations of the dedication and commitment of which young children are capable.

Clare was only 5 when her church began its first preparation course for children. The first group was of children aged 7 and over, but she came along, because her dad was helping to run the course, knowing that she was too young and wouldn't be allowed to receive Holy Communion yet. Nevertheless, she attended all the sessions, joining in all the activities and completing a workbook of her own. The following year she joined the 7-year-olds and completed the course all over again, with exactly the same degree of commitment, yet still too young to join the others at the altar rail. Clare finally received her Communion for the first time at the age of 7, after thoroughly completing the course for a third time! The leaders describe her as 'doggedly determined for God' and pray 'that her commitment never wavers'.

It's good for me

Elizabeth, after receiving the bread and wine for the first time, came to one of her leaders after the service and said: 'Ann, I don't like the taste of the wine, but I'll keep on drinking it, because I know it's good for me.' And she still is.

Who knows?

A 10-year-old approached the vicar one Sunday and told him she wanted to join the preparation group and begin receiving Communion. When the vicar spoke to her mother, a member of the congregation, to obtain her agreement, the mother expressed total disbelief that her daughter should be interested. Since being admitted to Communion, that girl has shown a strong commitment to faith in Christ.

Committed

Two 10-year-old boys with learning difficulties have been admitted to Communion in one parish and have shown a level of commitment to the church which surpasses that of many of the adult members. As well as attending regularly on Sunday mornings, they often attend the traditional evening services. Their parents have never attended church.

The monitoring group

A group was set up in the diocese consisting of the adviser in children's work and lay and clergy representatives from each of the parishes. The group had permission to set up a new scheme of work with children, admitting them to Communion around the age of 7 and encouraging them to Confirmation at a later age. The group was hosted by the parishes in turn and met about three times a year. It was able to:

- Provide a forum in which practical answers to questions could be shared. It addressed topics such as when would be a good time for the initial group of children to receive for the first time, who would come and talk to an open meeting at church about children and Communion, and whether parents should be invited to the preparation course sessions.
- Be a place to air the theological and pastoral issues, such as when the question of Confirmation should be raised with young adults; what possibilities there are for children or adults with learning difficulties; the question of children who were given a service of welcome as a baby, but who were not baptised; and what do we think Confirmation is now?
- Give opportunity for skills and work to be shared.

Initially each parish developed its own preparation course for children, ideas were then shared frequently in the group, and eventually an outline that could be offered to others as a starting point was distilled from those ideas.

Benefits and Problems

Parishes were asked to identify benefits and problems, and these are some of their comments:

Benefits

- They feel part of the church family, sharing in a common meal.
- The children begin to feel they are valuable within the congregation, and it gives them a great confidence boost.
- It seems to encourage their journey of faith.
- It is their opportunity to express their faith publicly.

- There is less of a tendency, having come in during the service, to fail to engage with it.
- The congregation is facing up to the implications of including children, seeing that they are truly part of the church.
- It says something to the congregation about 'coming as children' to Christ when they see committed children.
- Enthusiasm amongst younger children, knowing they will soon join in.
- There is more point to the church's policy of the children returning to the service after their group session if the service they return to is more all-age than exclusive.

Problems

- Several churches found it difficult to think of any!
- The Communion rail is too high to get the Communion cup over!
- Where children are not baptised and therefore are not admitted to Communion.
- Communicating members who miss two-thirds of the service.
- The lack of support from a very few parents who are not churchgoers themselves, to help their children to fulfil their commitment. Even if parents don't come to church they are usually very supportive and encouraging.

PART TWO

The Course

Introduction

This part of the book consists of a six-session course for children about Holy Communion. It has been written for groups of children aged 7 to 11 years to help them learn about belonging to God and appreciate the significance of Holy Communion in the life of a Christian. It is suitable for preparing children to receive Communion for the first time.

Using methods that the children will enjoy as well as learn from, each session points to part of the mystery of Holy Communion by focusing on one of the ways in which we belong to God, belong together and belong in the church family.

You will find in each of the six sessions a new aspect of the Communion to explore with ideas for starters, activities, stories, songs and prayers. There are also Talkabout take-home sheets linked to each session of the course, which can be photocopied free of charge for each child, so that they can compile a Communion pack of their own which documents their learning and provides a lasting memento of the course.

The sessions were originally devised, used and refined in those parishes in the Diocese of Southwell which have developed a pattern of nurture which involves admitting children to Communion prior to Confirmation. So, when these children completed the course, they received Holy Communion for the first time at a special service. Advice on using the course in this way is included on subsequent pages, but the material is adapted here to suit groups of children who will be learning about Communion, but not receiving it, as well as for those fortunate enough to be preparing for full participation.

There are many variations in understanding and practice within the Church of England, which all contribute to the richness of our understanding of the holy mystery which is Holy Communion. Differences exist from church to church and from communicant to communicant within any one congregation. These original parishes reflect a broad spectrum of traditions and we have tried to use words, pictures and ideas that will make our work acceptable in all traditions. Part of our intention is that this educational process will be a doorway into the tradition of your church. We also hope that it will allow a glimpse of the richness and the breadth of understanding which is held within the Anglican Church, because the Christian journey of these children may well take them on paths through traditions other than the one they are in now.

Notes for Leaders

- Overview
- Active learning
- Planning the sessions
- Prayer
- Preparation
- Talkabout take-home sheets
- Materials
- Other adults

Overview

Sessions 1 to 4

These take the theme of *Belonging* and offer ways to explore what belonging means and the different ways in which we belong to God. Ideally, if at all possible, between Sessions 1 and 2, the group will take part in a baptism in their own or a neighbouring church, or arrange for someone to demonstrate a baptism within Session 2.

Session 2

Why We Belong to God also has time for a look at each other's baptism certificates and a glance into the church register. The story is about Jesus and his friends. It is suggested that the group decorates a tablecloth together as a token of belonging and friendship.

Session 3

How We Belong to God offers a selection of signs and symbols to use as a puzzle or as the basis for a badge- or mobile-making activity. You will look at the caring and sharing activities of Jesus. The prayer section gives encouragement to pray for each other and other concerns.

Session 4

The Food of Belonging begins with a food quiz and the story of Jesus' last special meal with his friends. If you can arrange bread-making somehow, this is the time to do it.

Session 5

Ideally, this takes place in church and is designed to enable the children to become more familiar with the people who have special roles during a service of Holy Communion and the things they use during it. The priest, servers and others might get involved here.

Session 6

The final session is an opportunity for the children to express some of their thoughts and feelings, having taken part in a Communion service. A couple of adult communicants could join in this, so that the children hear a variety of reflections.

Active learning

Children of 7 learn most effectively by doing. Very little of what might be said to the children in the group will be retained, unless it is concise and reinforced by action on the child's part.

Children of 10 enjoy words more, have a growing ability to absorb ideas by listening and to learn by talking, but still do their most effective learning when they are doing something.

An action is central to the mystery that we call Holy Communion, Eucharist or the Mass. It is an action from which Christians learn throughout their lives. In these few sessions we hope children will engage in learning activities which give them a further glimpse of the importance and significance of Communion, associate it clearly and warmly with their belonging to God and enable them to take one or two of their own steps on the lifelong process of learning about Communion. This will be achieved if the learning material in this book is used to build a series of learning activities.

When the adult leader is talking it is usually a waste of children's learning time. The table at the top of the next page is a salutary

How information is received	Amount of information remembered after		
	3 hours	3 days	3 weeks
Reading	50%	5%	3%
Hearing	70%	10%	5%
Hearing and seeing	85%	65%	50%
Doing	95%	85%	70%

reminder. There are plenty of options in the sessions offered here. No group can do it all, but the hope is that leaders will be able to select a succession of activities that will allow the children to do, think and talk.

This table appears in the church children's workers training programme *Kaleidoscope*, published by Christian Education 1993.

A warning: having created a good learning environment and planned good learning activities, leaders can assume that children will learn, but they can't assume that what children will learn about belonging, Communion or church will take the form or use the language of the adult leaders. Leaders may be privileged to hear children talk about their ideas, but it is a mistake, especially in an area like Holy Communion where none of us have more than partial understanding, to try and impose an adult (in other words 'my') understanding on the children's experience. This is, of course, why it is so important for the children to have the experience itself.

Planning the sessions

A beginning, a middle and an end are needed for each session. Our topic is the most important thing the Christian family does together and the way the group is organised for these six meetings may take on a special flavour which reflects that.

The opening activity suggested each time makes sure all the children have said and done something early on. No one should be present for more than three or four minutes without contributing.

You may like to follow your usual opening pattern of greeting, prayer or song, or you may use the opening greeting from your church's Communion service. If you decide to make the tablecloth described in Session 2, you could add laying the table to your opening.

The middle of our sessions focuses on God-centred activity, and while we have assumed you have about 45 minutes with your group, you will probably need to adjust it to fit the available time. Don't feel you have to do everything.

The ending is a time of prayer.

Prayer

Prayer must be part of the life of any group of Christians, and it must be a living part. Using one of the prayer suggestions at the end of each session may be a helpful variation in your group's usual pattern of prayer, and a reminder not to pray on behalf of the children, but to use ways into prayer that enable them to approach God themselves.

Prayer can be active or passive; it can be vocal, musical or silent, formal or informal, moving or stationary; it can use symbols, pictures, actions or familiar objects. In these learning sessions in particular, it must strike the children as enjoyable and useful. Variety and participation will be essential.

Preparation

The sacrifice of valuable leader time to attend preparation meetings is necessary, as it makes a difference to the effectiveness of the learning that takes place in the group.

As well as the usual task of working out which part of this material to use and who takes responsibility for leading each part of each session, the leaders are encouraged to begin the preparation by discussing the questions below.

- Why is receiving Holy Communion important to me?
- Why is it important to children?
- What prayers, responses, songs, hymns, and customs from our Communion service can be of benefit during this topic?
- Does our Communion service need to change, so that children can participate more?

Talkabout take-home sheets

There are Talkabout take-home sheets associated with each session (except the last). You may make as many photocopies as you need for the children in your group, free of charge.

As their name implies, these pages are designed to encourage talking. Whether you talk together before putting anything on the sheets or talk as you draw and write, they should provide a means of getting everyone thinking and speaking. Make sure the sheets aren't a burden to any of the children. Some of them won't enjoy writing and some of them may not be too keen on drawing, so it will be especially important for them to understand that they are something to talk about, not test papers to be completed faultlessly.

You may decide not to use them all, especially in Session 1, as you will not have time to tackle everything. However, by the end of Session 5 each child should have a complete set. Some of the sheets are fairly self-explanatory and the children may be able to complete them at home; this will also give the parents an opportunity to help and to talk about what the group has been doing.

Talkabout sheet 5, *Living Stones*, also offers the opportunity to encourage the children to talk to adult members of the congregation. They will do this by asking for names to go on the stones and perhaps an additional piece of information, such as how long they have been a member of their current church, or whether they have belonged to any other church.

If you can provide the children with a means of keeping the Talkabout sheets in good condition until the end of the course, perhaps an envelope or a plastic wallet, they can then be bound into book form and kept as a permanent reminder of their learning in these sessions and of all the people in the group. The *My Communion Pack* title page can be photocopied on to card to provide a cover and slide binders are available from any source of office supplies – or your local school or diocesan resource centre might be able to assist with comb binding.

Materials

Here is a summary of what you might need for each session. It will vary according to which of the suggested activities you select. Your Christian bookshop, diocesan adviser or resource centre may be able to help with any difficulties.

For all sessions

The story
Pencils, felt pens and/or coloured pencils.
A flip chart, white board or large sheets of paper will often be helpful to record as well as to focus discussions.

Songs
Check with the school(s) attended by the children to discover what they may be familiar with. The following books are all recommended:

Big Blue Planet (Methodist Publishing House, 1995)

The Children's Hymn Book (Kevin Mayhew, 1997)

Complete Anglican Hymns Old and New (Kevin Mayhew, 2000)

Easy to Play Children's Favourite Hymns and Songs (Kevin Mayhew, 2001)

Feeling Good: Songs of Wonder and Worship for Fives and Under (NS/Church House Publishing, 1994)

Jump Up If You're Wearing Red! (NS/Church House Publishing, 1996)

Kidsource and *Kidsource 2* (Kevin Mayhew, 1999 and 2002)

Let's All Clap Hands and *Let's Sing and Shout* (Scripture Union, 2003)

Praying in Song (Kevin Mayhew, 2000)

Prayer

Whatever written prayers, objects for meditation, books you have decided to use.

Session 1

- Talkabout sheets 1 to 5.
- Starter game.
- Photoboard: board, photographs, glue, photographer?
- Story: The birth of Jesus or Jesus and the children (Matthew 18).

Session 2

- Talkabout sheets 6 to 8.
- Spare baptism certificates.
- Mirror card – an optional extra for Talkabout sheet 6.
- Story: Jesus calls the disciples (Matthew 4:18-22) or Zacchaeus (Luke 19:1-10) or *Water* in the Teddy Horsley series published by Christian Education, 1996.
- Tablecloth.
- Fabric crayons or fabric paints.
- Books of prayers for children.

Session 3

- Talkabout sheets 9 to 13.
- Blank card badges or badge machine for symbol badges.
- Story: *Jesus Gives the People Food* (Lion Story Bible) or similar.
- Bread and wine.
- Bibles and service books for Talkabout sheet 11.
- Mobiles: coat hangers or wooden crosspieces, card, cotton, decorative paper or material.

Session 4

- Talkabout sheet 14.
- A selection of foods to be tasted; a blindfold.
- Story: The Last Supper (Matthew 26:26-29); Teddy Horsley *The Picnic* (Christian Education).
- Celebratory food – an Easter egg or birthday cake, for example.

Session 5

- Talkabout sheet 15.
- In church: all the Communion vessels, etc., some of the people who help at Communion (priest, server, musician, etc.). Bread and wine.

Session 6

- Paper.
- Paint/crayons/felt tips.
- A variety of collage materials.
- Clay.

Other adults

The children are part of the congregation and are learning about belonging. As part of the learning they will be encouraged to get to know some more adult members of their congregation. It will help if the adult members are doing some learning about Holy Communion and belonging at the same time. It may be possible to discuss how this might be achieved by joint planning of sermons, adult study groups, youth groups, etc. as well as using displays, the magazine, and the children taking special roles in the service during this preparation period.

All this will provide additional opportunities for children to hear adults talk about their faith and the part receiving Holy Communion plays in their lives. It will also make it easier to avoid giving the impression that everyone thinks the same or that it is only the children in the church community who do any learning and have any work to display or present. Suggestions for reading and study are given in *Other Resources* on page 44; further ideas and other help will be available from your diocesan advisers.

Session 1
Belonging to God

Aims

- To think about the groups we belong to.
- To look at our family, our church family and Jesus' family.
- To see baptism as a sign of our belonging.

It is easy in a group like this to assume that everyone knows each other, but they probably don't all know everybody else. Time spent on an opening activity that gives the group (adults and children) a chance to learn and use everyone's name and perhaps to find out something new about each other is a good investment.

Starter

Names

Try a game that uses names, such as *spin the plate*, or borrow a badge-making machine and let everyone make a name badge that shows their name and something about them.

To play *spin the plate*, everyone sits in a circle – on chairs or on the floor. Then everyone says their name. One person in the centre of the circle spins a large plate (or round wooden breadboard) shouts out the name of someone present and they have to catch it before it falls. If they do, they get to spin it next. If they don't, the original 'spinner' has to do it again . . .

If you can borrow a parachute the right size for the group, try this game. Choose one person to stand in the middle underneath it, while the rest of the group is evenly spaced around the edge of the parachute, holding it at waist height. Everyone then raises their arms to lift the parachute in the air and once it's up in the air they shout someone else's name and try to change places with them before the parachute comes down and lands on top of them. Now the person whose name was called does the same and so on – but the person in the middle can't call a name that has been used already.

Activity

What groups do you belong to?

Talk about the groups you are each part of. Let each child mention at least one, and make a list of all the groups mentioned on a big sheet of paper as you talk. This group list could be used as part of a display in church. Ask someone to come and photograph the children and the groups referred to, if you can, and build up a photoboard to use in church, either on its own or as part of a larger display.

Talkabout take-home sheets

My families

Talkabout sheets 1, 2, 3 and 4 form part of this session. Use one or two while you are all together and ask for the others to be completed at home with a little help from parents.

Talkabout sheet 1, *All About Me*, is straightforward. Ask everyone (including the leader and any adults) to draw their family on Talkabout sheet 2. Talk as you draw, and remember that everyone's family will be different and that most children are fairly matter-of-fact about what their family is like. Leaders must, of course, affirm everyone, must not express surprise or be judgemental, and should not invade family privacy. Be prepared to answer for yourself any question you ask the children. You may like to do this exercise about the school family instead or as well (see Talkabout sheet 3).

On Talkabout sheet 4 draw your church. There will need to be a little discussion of who is in our church family, but each child should focus on whichever aspect of 'church' is most real, and expect each child's list to be different.

Story

Jesus was born into a family

Tell the story of the birth of Jesus in your own words or using a storybook, or let the children remember the story between them.

or

Jesus and the children

Tell the story of Jesus, putting a child in the midst of the disciples to show who is the greatest (Matthew 18). Make a list of what is good about being children. Work out some things adults could do to be like them.

Song

If you have used the Christmas story, sing a favourite Christmas song or carol, whatever time of year it is, or use *I Am The Church* (Jump Up).

Closing activity

Signs of belonging

Anglicans recognise two sacraments as particularly important – baptism and Holy Communion. They are both signs that we belong to Christ. Ask children to bring a baptism certificate next week. If you have a little time now, find out who has been baptised and discuss what happens at a baptism.

Share a little bread and wine of the sort that is used at your Communion service, so that the children have a first idea of what it tastes like.

Before next time

Part of the congregation

It would be good for the children to find out a little more about one or two people in the church. They could ask what they do at church, whether they been baptised, and if so when and where, how long have they been coming to this church, etc. Talkabout sheet 5, *Living Stones*, is designed to help this process. Children could open a conversation with one of the adults by asking them to sign their name in a stone on the sheet, perhaps adding the year of their baptism. It could usefully take three or four weeks to complete the whole sheet, especially if you add extra stones.

Ask the children and the adults to bring their baptism certificate next time, and a photograph taken on the day they were baptised, if they can.

Closing prayer

Close the session with a time of quiet.

If your group is used to silence or you want to help it use silence through this course, play some quiet music and place a candle, bread and wine centrally as a focus for one minute of silent meditation. (If this is new to the group, start with a shorter period and build it up each week.)

Sit quietly in the circle and slowly name each child and adult, so that the rest can silently pray for them, as well as remembering who they are.

Read, or say together, the Kyries – Lord have mercy . . . (*Common Worship*, Order 1, page 170).

Say the Grace together.

Session 2

Why We Belong to God

Aims

- To think about some of the friends of Jesus.
- To see ourselves as friends of Jesus.
- To pray for each other.

Starter

Baptism certificates

Look at each other's baptism certificates, and have some spares available for those who don't have one. Look at the church baptism register for any of the children who were baptised here, other family members, people with the same name, etc.

Demonstrate a baptism at the font or in a bowl, asking the children to remember what they have seen and heard at baptisms.

Activity

Talkabout sheet 6

We belong to God because God loves us. God knows us all by name. Look at Talkabout sheet 6. Share a few thoughts on who God loves and then complete the sheet by inviting the group to put their own name on first and then asking every other member of the group to write their name on each other's sheet. You could supply small pieces of mirror card to be stuck on the sheet as a reminder that God loves 'me'.

Story

Friends of Jesus

We belong to God because God wants us to be friends of Jesus. Tell the story of Jesus calling the fishermen (Matthew 4:18-22) or how he went to eat at the house of Zacchaeus (Luke 19:1-10). There are puzzles about the disciples' names and nicknames on Talkabout sheet 7.

Alternatively, use the Teddy Horsley story *Water* (by L. Francis and N. Slee, published by Christian Education, 1996), in which Teddy Horsley observes the qualities of water and then experiences the water of baptism.

Activity

Jesus eats with his friends

Mention the way this group has a drink and biscuit/cake together each time it meets (if it does!) and the Communion shared by the church all around the world each week. The Communion table has a special cloth and so perhaps should this group . . .

Decorate a tablecloth for this group's refreshment time or for its working table. Use fabric crayons on a piece of white material. Ask everyone to put their name and maybe a picture of themselves or a picture of something they like or are good at. You may be able to identify a symbol for the whole group – if so this could be drawn in the middle. Put a picture of a font, bread and wine, the church building and whatever else seems appropriate. Then you can add things as you go through the course.

Song

Sing a song about belonging or friendship such as:

Jesus' love is very wonderful

Zacchaeus was a very little man

Everyone matters to Jesus

Closing activity

We belong to God . . . because we pray together

Make sure everyone has filled in the names of your group on Talkabout sheet 6 and try and remember to pray for each other during the week – every day if you can!

Before next time

Favourite prayers

Find a favourite prayer of your own or of a family or church member, if you can. Lend the children some books of children's prayers from the church library or children's corner if they are unlikely to have access to them at home.

or

Talkabout sheet 8

Talkabout sheet 8 *Signs of Belonging* can be tackled at home during the time before the next meeting.

Closing prayer

Have a short time of quiet, with space for children to pray both silently and out loud. If your group is learning to use silent prayer through this course, play some quiet music and place a candle, bread and wine on your tablecloth as a focus for one minute (or shorter) of silent meditation.

Read the Sanctus – Holy, holy, holy . . . (*Common Worship*, Order 1, page 176).

Session 3

How We Belong to God

Aim

- To consider things we and others do that show we belong to God.

Starter

We belong . . . by coming to church

Begin by brainstorming a list entitled 'What I like about coming to church.' Make sure everyone contributes something and avoid discussing contributions (if possible). Just put everything and anything on the list. Then have a go at Talkabout sheet 9 together. When you have worked out what links with school, church and home, see if you can think of four or five other celebrations that happen at church and add them in the space round the church building.

Activity

We belong . . . by having signs and badges

Look at the road sign quiz on Talkabout sheet 10. See how many you can work out.

There are some Christian symbols there too, so discuss what they are. Talk about where you might have seen them.

Enlarge these symbols and use them to make mobiles or make badges for yourselves.

Story

We belong . . . by sharing and caring

Who needs caring for at the moment? Make a note to include any situations or people mentioned in your prayers at the end. Jesus very often showed his care for people who were in need. You could put up a prayer list at the beginning of each session from now on, and check what everyone's concerns and thanksgivings are each time.

Tell the story of the Feeding of the Five Thousand in your own words or using *Jesus Gives the People Food* (Lion Story Bible). Talk with the children about the story and when sharing is easy and when it is hard. Something may arise out of this discussion for your prayer list.

Activity

We belong . . . by remembering Jesus

We remember Jesus in Holy Communion.

Tell the story of the Last Supper, in your own words. Break some bread together round the table and remember that Jesus told us to do this as a way of remembering him, by saying, 'This is my body . . .'. You should be able to bring to mind one or two things each that it is important to remember, and also different ways of remembering them – mementos, hugs, cards, stick-on notes, and many, many more. The photograph album often has a great fascination for most children and many adults, so bringing one to the group would be a good illustration.

One of the great things about Holy Communion is that it helps us remember what Jesus was and did. Talkabout sheet 11 helps you take this a little further.

Closing activity

We belong . . . by talking and listening to God

Look at the favourite prayers that have been brought. Decide which one you could use today.

Write a new one now or at home.

Talk with the children and leaders about how and when they pray. If you have a church library or children's corner look at the books of prayers available there.

One or two children may like to learn a prayer. The Kyries make a good choice. There is space on Talkabout sheet 12, *Prayers,* to write your favourite prayer or to make up one of your own.

If you have time make a prayer mobile or a prayer cube. Prayer cubes can have a grace on each side and be rolled before the meal to choose a grace, similarly with prayers to end a meeting, or with names of members of the group. A mobile can be hung with cards bearing a prayer on one side and a decorative design on the other. A larger card on a long string in the middle might have on one side 'Lord, in your mercy', and on the other 'Hear our prayer', or whichever response is customary in your church.

Song

Choose a quiet song the children know and like.

Closing prayer

Do the *Hand prayer* as outlined on Talkabout sheet 13.

If your group is learning to use silent prayer through this course, play some quiet music and place a candle, a bowl of water and some of the photos on your tablecloth as a focus for one minute (or shorter) of silent meditation.

Read the Agnus Dei – the version you use in church – Lamb of God . . . / Jesus, Lamb of God . . . (*Common Worship,* Order 1, page 179).

Close the session with the Grace.

Session 4
The Food of Belonging

Aim

- To enjoy and talk about special food.

Starter

Start with a food-tasting quiz. Prepare a selection of foods for the children to taste. Go for variety, but make sure that several will have associations for them. (Make sure not to offend anyone's dietary customs or allergies – and avoid nuts.) Include things like Easter egg, birthday cake, pickled onion, honey, tomato ketchup, salt, etc., but also reflect the cultures and customs of your area.

Let the children taste the foods blindfolded, one at a time. They can either do this in another room, so they can comment on each individual food as they taste it, or, if the foods themselves are concealed everyone can listen to each other's comments as they taste them (although this runs the risk of someone blurting out what it is). Ask the children if the food (either its taste or its smell) reminds them of something. Some of the foods may remind individuals of particular occasions, days of the week, celebrations, etc. or they may be able to remember the last time they had that food. What sort of memories does the food bring back – ordinary or special, good or bad?

Activity

Do the quiz on Talkabout sheet 14, *Food of Belonging,* about foods that belong to special occasions or people. List other special occasion foods if you can.

Story

Read *The Picnic* from the Teddy Horsley series and talk about what happens in the story.

The Passover

Tell the story of the Last Supper in the Upper Room, the special last meal that Jesus had with his friends (Matthew 26:26-29). Jesus wanted his friends to know how special they were to him so they celebrated on this special day of Passover with a meal together.

You may have time to explore the story behind the Passover celebration and the special food that is eaten then. You will find information and / or people to help you with this in local schools, libraries, synagogues, Council of Christians and Jews groups, libraries or contact your diocesan advisers.

Activity

Tell the group that Jesus wanted his friends to remember him and the way he gave his life for them. Ask how Jesus wanted them to do this. Several good answers may emerge but follow one that mentions bread and wine and the way that reminds us of Jesus. Draw out explanation and understanding from the children, rather than trying to give an adult rationalisation. This powerful story will stimulate their thinking, and give them an opportunity to reflect on what they have heard in earlier sessions of this course.

Song

Choose a song about food or favourite things such as:

I like eating (Jump Up)

Before next time

If you can, arrange some bread-making. This may be an opportunity to involve a parent or member of the congregation who bakes regularly. Alternatively use a breadmaker or a bread mix of the 'just add water' variety.

Closing prayer

If your group is learning to use silent prayer through this course, play some quiet music and place a candle and some of the food on your tablecloth as a focus for one minute (or shorter) of silent meditation or whatever has become your pattern.

Encourage the group to mention any recent or coming celebrations.

Read the Eucharistic Prayer which your church uses.

Close the session with the Grace.

Session 5
In Church

Aim

- To become familiar with Communion in your church.

This is a practical session, which takes place in church and gives the children an opportunity to show what they know about what goes on in their Communion service and to practise receiving the bread and wine.

Starter

In remembrance

Remembrance has in it the idea of making the person or event real again. As we gather for Holy Communion we re-enact the Last Supper. Gather round your bare altar table for five minutes at the beginning of this session and remember between you who might have been there the first time. Piece together the story of what happened. Wonder together about how it would have been. Use your imaginations – the Gospel account doesn't mention everyone who was there nor does it tell of every little thing that took place. How did Peter feel? How did Jesus feel? What did they think when Jesus broke the bread? If you like, share bread and wine as they did and talk about how you feel.

Song

Ask the children to choose their favourite Communion song or sing *As we are gathered* (Complete Anglican Hymns Old and New).

Activity

What's missing?

Having removed all the usual things from the altar table and surrounds, now ask the children to identify what is missing, as each item is mentioned, bring it back, commenting on what it is there for.

Ask the children if there is anything they wonder about.

If there are usually people in the sanctuary with particular jobs to do, invite them to this session so that they can play their part.

If your church uses a home Communion set, this may be a good way to introduce the children to the idea that many Christians will want to receive Communion at home or in hospital if they can't get to church. You may be able to name individuals who have home Communions at the moment.

Use Talkabout sheet 15 to review the objects and people you have named.

Taste and see

Let the children taste the sort of bread and wine that you use at your Communion services, especially if they haven't tasted it at all yet. Explain simply how they are made.

Practise receiving the bread and wine in the usual way.

Ask if there is anything the children want to know.

Ask if any of the children (or adults) have anything they want to say.

Ready for next time

Make sure everyone has a full set of Talkabout take-home sheets.

Arrange to collect them all and bind them. Decide if they will be on display in church and when they may be collected or presented. Avoid making the sheets a burden for any of the children.

Closing prayer

If your group is learning to use silent prayer through this course, play some quiet music, light the candles on the altar and sit or stand around it for one minute (or shorter) of silent meditation.

Pray for each member of the group by name.

Read the Prayer of Humble Access you use in church – We do not presume . . . Most merciful Lord . . . (*Common Worship*, Order 1, page 181).

Close the session with the Grace.

Session 6
My Communion

Aim

- To hear how the children experience Communion, to give them time to wonder and reflect, and to let the children hear from two adults about the significance of Communion for them.

Ideally all the children will have attended a service of Holy Communion in the time between Session 5 and this session. If this results in a gap between the sessions, this is no bad thing.

The important thing is to sustain a comfortable conversation which enables each person present to share a little about what a Communion service was like for them, knowing the rest of the group will be keen to hear from them, not commenting on their experience or expecting it to be the same as anyone else's.

You may invite two adult members of the church to join the group for this session – people the children will easily feel comfortable with (and vice versa) as you are only together for this one session. Alternatively, the adults leading the course may take this role, but resist the typical adult role of one who comments, corrects or adds information to a child's contribution. You could invite the parents, too, and turn the session into a celebration for the last meeting of this group.

Starter

Give time for introductions if new adults have joined the group for this session.

Play the same game you used in Session 1 if you enjoyed it.

Activity

Remembering

It may help to meet where the Communion took place, or to have bread and wine present on your tablecloth in your normal meeting place. With the aid of some quiet music, cast your minds back to the last time you were in a Communion service, remember what you saw – the sounds, the smell, walking towards the Communion table, being handed the bread and/or seeing it handed to others, walking away.

Initiate some 'wondering' questions.

Build a word picture of your feelings and thoughts on a large sheet of paper – or on your tablecloth – taking it in turns (to start with at least) to offer a word.

Now break into small groups and take it in turns to talk and wonder about the Communion service and your thoughts and feelings.

And finally encourage everyone (yes, adults and children) to put their thoughts and feelings into a drawing, a painting, an arrangement of flowers, shells and pebbles or a clay model.

Closing activity

Have a silent walk. With some quiet background music, walk silently round the room to look at everyone's drawing, painting or model.

Stand in a circle and share short comments about what you found interesting or good in any of the creations.

Song

Choose a favourite from the course, or any one the children enjoy singing.

Closing prayer

If your group has been learning to use silent prayer through this course, play some quiet music and place a candle, some bread and wine and the participants' artwork, if you can, as a focus for one minute of silent meditation, or whatever has become your pattern.

Read, or say together, the Lord's Prayer.

Close the session with the Grace, the Communion service prayer or time of quiet. Encourage the group to say thank you for anything good.

Finish with the dismissal or the blessing from the Communion service.

Final thoughts

A display of pictures and comments could usefully be mounted in church or wherever members of the congregation will see it, but first check that everyone is happy for their creative work to be used in this way.

If your church has changed or is considering changing its policy on admitting children to Communion, a (no-names) résumé of this session may form a helpful contribution to the discussions about change or to the monitoring of any new pattern.

Collect the Talkabout take-home sheets and firm up collection or presentation arrangements.

Other Resources and Further Reading

Background

Tuesday's Child, edited by John Sutcliffe, a reader for Christian Educators – contains sections on many out-of-print reports and books (Christian Education, 2001).

On the Way, a report on the whole question of patterns of initiation in parishes (CHP, 1994).

Children and Holy Communion, an Ecumenical Consideration amongst Churches in Britain and Ireland by the British Council of Churches Consultative Group on Ministry among Children (British Council of Churches, 1989).

Communion before Confirmation, a report on the experiments in Peterborough, Manchester and Southwark dioceses (Culham College Institute, 1993).

Children in Communion (Grove Worship Series No 112, 1990).

Children and Communion, the Knaresborough Report, out of print, (see above) – a readable summary of the historical, theological and practical issues (CHP, 1985).

Children in Worship: Congregations in Bloom by Caroline Fairless (Church Publishing Inc, NY, 2000).

Let the Children Come to Communion by Stephen Lake (SPCK, 2006).

Offering the Gospel to Children by Gretchen Wolff Pritchard (Cowley, 1992).

Young Children and Worship by Sonia Stewart and Jerome Berryman (The Westminster Press, 1990).

The Spirit of the Child by David Hay/Rebecca Nye (Jessica Kingsley, revised edition, 2006).

Resources

Welcome To The Lord's Table by Margaret Withers (BRF, 1999).

Come And Join The Celebration by Betty Pedley and John Muir (National Society/ Church House Publishing).

My Communion Book – A Child's Guide to Holy Communion by Diana Murrie (Church House Publishing, 2002).

The Communion Cube by Diana Murrie and Margaret Withers (Church House Publishing, 2002).

Blessed Be God for Ever (The Church in Wales, 2002).

Bread For All God's Family by Leslie Francis and Diane Dayson (Gracewing, 1997).

Share by Nick Harding (Kevin Mayhew, 2002).

Teddy Horsley The Picnic (Holy Communion) and *Water* (Baptism) from a series by Leslie Francis and Nicola Slee, in which the church-going bear builds bridges between day-to-day experiences and major Christian themes (Christian Education, 1996).

Roots – learning material for every Sunday of the year, including suggestions for worship with all ages, based on the Revised Common Lectionary. Contact: Roots Subscriptions, 4 John Wesley Road, Peterborough, PE4 6ZP.
Tel: 01733 325 002.
Email: sales@mph.org.uk
www.rootsontheweb.com

Seasons Of The Spirit – Lectionary-based all-age worship and learning materials.
Tel: 0131 229 3776
www.spiritseasons.com

PART THREE

My Communion Pack

MY COMMUNION PACK

NAME ....

Talkabout

Take-home sheets

Complete these sheets in the group or at home.

Keep them in a folder, binder or scrapbook.

Decorate the cover.
Don't forget to put your name on!

When you have finished all the sheets,
keep them safe. You can add other things -
prayers, pictures or readings - to make this
your own special book about Holy Communion.

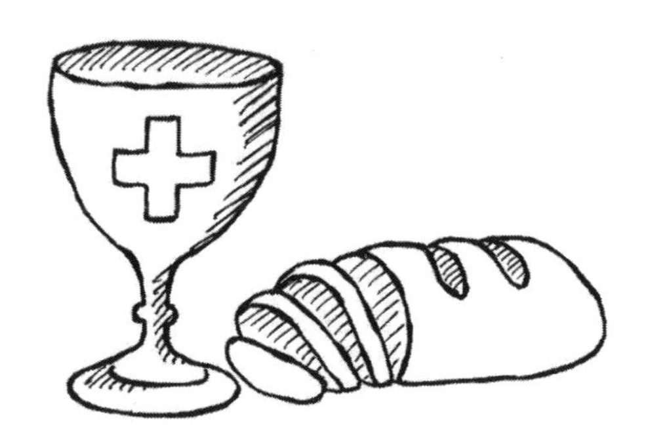

All About Me

This is me

(draw yourself or stick a photo here)

My name is

My birthday is on

I am ☐ years old

I live at

My favourite person is

My favourite food is

What makes me laugh

What makes me happy

What makes me sad

I Belong . . . in my family

Sheet 2

This is my family

(draw them or stick a photo here)

These are their names

Things I do at home

(draw or write or both)

I came into my family on

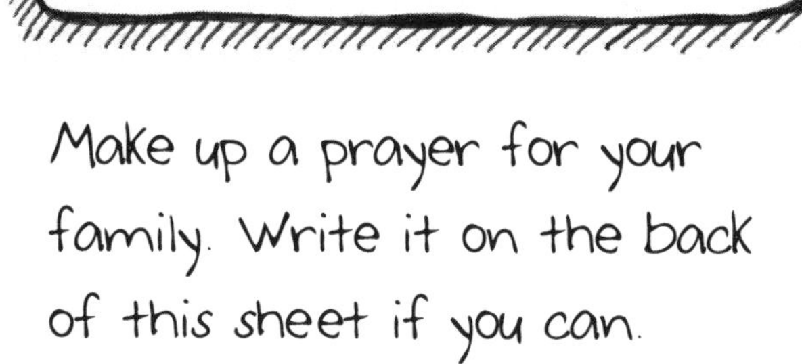

Make up a prayer for your family. Write it on the back of this sheet if you can.

I Belong . . . in my school

Sheet 3

My school is called

My teacher is

I am in class

I am good at

My best friend at school is

What we do together
(draw or write or both)

I am not so good at

If you like drawing, you can do a picture on the back of this sheet. Why not draw your school, your friend or your teacher?

I Belong . . . in my church

Sheet 4

This is my church

(draw it or stick a photo here)

It is called

There are lots of people in our church family. Here are some of their names

Things I do at church
(draw or write or both)

Do you belong anywhere else, such as Brownies, Cubs or a club?

Living Stones

Write your name on one of the stones in the wall.

Each week at church ask a grown-up
to write their name on a stone.

St Peter in his Epistle calls us 'living' stones.

What do you think he means?

You can find it in the Bible, 1 Peter chapter 2, verse 4.

God Loves me

God knows me by my name.

God knows my family by their names.

God knows all the people in my church by their names.

God knows all my friends in this group.

Here are their names.

GOD LOVES THEM ALL TOO!

Names

My name is

Sheet 7

Names are a special sign of belonging.

Write your family name here

What is your best friend's family name?

Here are the jumbled-up names of some of Jesus' friends. Can you work out what they are?

TREEP

HiPPiL

SMEAJ

NOMiS

NOHJ

Find out the names of the rest of Jesus' disciples. Write them here.

Can you jumble up your name to make other words?

Some of Jesus' friends had nicknames – Peter was 'the Rock', James and John 'the sons of thunder'. Why do you think they were given these names?

Do you or your friends have nicknames? What are they?

If you could choose another name for yourself, what would it be?

Signs of Belonging

Badges are a sign of belonging - Cubs, Brownies, football clubs.
Does your school have a badge? Draw some badges here.

In baptism, the sign of the cross is used. How many different kinds of cross can you find?
Draw or cut and stick them here.

Can you fill in the missing letters to make the right word?

I was **b** _ _ _ into the world.

I **s** _ _ _ _ _ _ school.

I am **b** _ _ _ _ _ _ _ into the Church.

Celebration

Here are things we celebrate at home, at school and in church. Draw a line from each word to the right place. Some can be celebrated in more than one place, so use more than one line!

Christmas

wedding

leaving school

Mothering Sunday

School

birthdays

baptism

new job

Eucharist

Christingle

end of term

Church

passing exams

carol service

Holy Communion

new baby

anniversary

Home

Harvest

retirement

Easter

Signs and Symbols

Do you know what these signs mean?

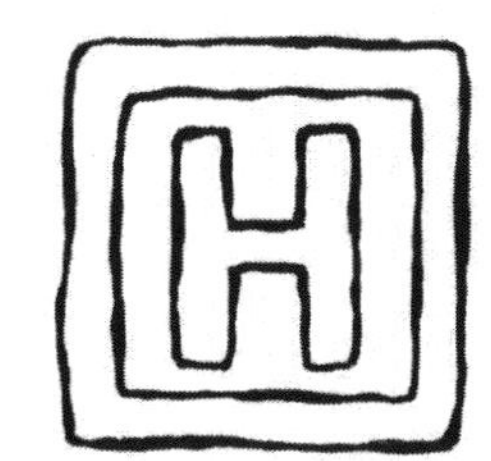

(plus any others you can think of!)

Can you find any signs and symbols like this in your church?
What do you think they are signs of?

Do This in Remembrance of Me

Remembering things is an important part of our lives. We keep things to remind ourselves of important and happy events. Do you have remembering things at home – a baby book or photograph album? What does your family keep?

In church we remember things too. What is there in your church to remind you of people and past events?

In the Communion service we remember the Last Supper and the death of Jesus on the cross.

Here are some words for the breaking of the bread. Which words does your church use?

Draw a ring round them.

Holy Communion **Eucharist** **Mass** **the Lord's Supper**

Can you put these words in the right spaces?

gave **broke** **took** **blessed**

Jesus _ _ _ _ the bread. He _ _ _ _ _ _ _ it,

he _ _ _ _ _ it and _ _ _ _ it to them.

You can find the story in the Bible, Mark chapter 14

This is part of the Communion service. Watch and listen for it. See if you can find the remembering words in your church service book.

Prayers

Use the prayer on this page to start a collection of prayers in a notebook. You can write your own if you wish. Here is one to begin with. You can use them in the morning, at night, or any time.

A prayer for little things

Dear God,
I bring to you
all the little things on earth:
a feather,
a daisy,
a marble,
a ladybird . . .
They are all your special treasures,
as we are your special treasures.
May we all be beautiful for you
each in our own way,
giving thanks for your infinite care
of the tiniest things.

Christopher Herbert, *Prayers for Children*
National Society/Church House Publishing, 1993

When You Pray . . .

Draw round your hand on a piece of paper like this:

There are five different kinds of prayer. Each finger can help you to remember the names. They are

praise **saying sorry** **asking** **thanking** **silent prayer**

You can also use your fingers to remind you of different things to pray for, like this

thumb this is the **strongest** finger. Pray for all the strong things in your life, like home and family, that protect and take care of you.

index the **pointing** finger. Pray for all those who guide and help, like teachers, clergy, doctors, fire and police services.

middle this is the **tallest** finger. Pray for all those who have power in the world.

ring this is the **weakest** finger. It cannot do much by itself. Pray for the poor, weak and helpless.

little the **smallest** and **last** finger. Pray for yourself.

When you say your prayers, hold each finger in turn, and remember!

Food of Belonging

Can you match the food on the left to the words on the right?

birthday cake	China
the Last Supper	Christmas
fish	India
mince pies	Italy
eggs	Holy Communion
bread and wine	Fridays
spaghetti	Easter
curry	birthday
chow mein	Maundy Thursday

Here are some **Communion** words for you to find.

Do you know what they all mean? Don't worry if you don't!

communion
eucharist
bread
wine
chalice
paten
consecrate
water
altar
take
eat
draw
near
break
wafer

e	u	c	h	a	r	i	s	t	b	e	c
d	f	o	g	h	e	b	g	a	k	d	i
w	i	n	e	r	t	a	n	a	s	b	e
a	p	s	v	w	a	l	t	a	r	r	h
f	z	e	f	a	w	r	d	e	b	e	g
e	r	c	f	a	w	r	a	e	b	a	g
r	v	r	e	s	r	k	w	a	r	d	q
a	p	a	t	e	n	r	e	b	n	g	r
b	y	t	r	s	o	r	d	l	e	m	n
t	h	e	a	t	n	a	p	s	u	w	b
c	h	a	l	i	c	e	n	a	e	c	d
m	e	p	n	o	i	n	u	m	m	o	c

Things We Use . . .

Which of these things do you use in your church's Communion service? Put a ring round the words.

cross	**candles**	**chalice**	**paten**	**ciborium**
lavabo bowl	**plate**	**cup**	**flagon**	**holy table**
altar	**chasuble**	**stole**	**surplice**	**burse**
cassock	**purificator**	**acolyte**	**service book**	**microphone**
bookstand	**priest**	**server**	**crucifer**	**water**
wine	**wafers**	**bread**	**priest's wafer**	**alb**

Here is a Communion picture for you to colour.

How is this the same as your church?
How is it different?